YOUR KNOWLEDGE HAS VALUE

- We will publish your bachelor's and
  master's thesis, essays and papers

- Your own eBook and book -
  sold worldwide in all relevant shops

- Earn money with each sale

Upload your text at www.GRIN.com
and publish for free

Dominik Heinz

Employee Development Using Social Media Tools

GRIN Publishing

Imprint:

Copyright © 2009 GRIN Verlag, Open Publishing GmbH
Print and binding: Books on Demand GmbH, Norderstedt Germany
ISBN: 978-3-656-14909-5

This book at GRIN:

http://www.grin.com/en/e-book/190433/employee-development-using-social-media-tools

GRIN - Your knowledge has value

Since its foundation in 1998, GRIN has specialized in publishing academic texts by students, college teachers and other academics as e-book and printed book. The website www.grin.com is an ideal platform for presenting term papers, final papers, scientific essays, dissertations and specialist books.

Visit us on the internet:

http://www.grin.com/

http://www.facebook.com/grincom

http://www.twitter.com/grin_com

Assignment

Employee Development Using
Social Media Tools

Master of Business Administration (MBA)

Module: Human Resource Management

Author: Dominik M. Heinz

Stuttgart, December 16th 2009

I.   Content

II.   Introduction

The backbone of a company is the body of its employees. It is a company's body of employees striving for excellence that strengthens a company's overall success. Today, the markets are getting harder; money is lost in large financial crises and the pressure on every company's management staff is increasing. It is crucial, maybe more than ever, to have employees who are not only well trained but who can also act and develop quick, as well as easily adapt new business areas or departments within the company's range. Intelligence, collaboration and excellent performance are needed – qualities which are enhanced by social web tools.

III.   Executive Summary

This assignment summarizes the most important aspects of the topic employee development within the human resource management area, and shows whether the task employee development can be improved when performed with the support of social media tools. Social media tools are interactive, often web based tools which help individual employees to manage their knowledge, connect with each other, and communicate. This assignment will show the immensely positive impact of social media tools in specifically employee development and training processes.

IV.   Abbreviations

1   T & D – Training and Development
2   HiPo – High Potential
3   HiPer – High Performer
4   KM – Knowledge Management

1   Definitions

1.1   Applied Terminology

- Social Media: collective content created by any individual of that collective;
- Social Media tools: tools that help individuals collaborate, communicate, and access their collective content;
- Employee Development: in this paper, the term "employee development" is used for both an overall term for employee development, training, education, and ramp-up, as well as a special term indicating a focus on employee development toward a future job;
- Intranet: websites only accessible within a company's network;

2   Social Media

2.1   Definition

The term "Social Media Tools" describes websites and tools that rely on people, who are using them in an interactive manner. The content is not being provided by a super user, but by the normal users themselves. Everybody using a social media tool is part of the creation process. The usage change of internet based tools and websites from a read-only way to this interactive style has been labeled as the change from "Web 1.0" to "Web 2.0". However, the term "Web 2.0" has never been completely accepted within business circles. As a matter of fact, the usage of the term is decreasing.[1]

Today the term "Social Media Tools" is used. L. Safko and D. Brake define three basic rules concerning social media:

1. Social Media is all about enabling conversations;
2. You cannot control conversations, but you can influence them;
3. Influence is the bedrock upon which all economically viable relationships are built;[2]

2.2   History

Toward the year 2000, internet businesses and offerings grew overwhelmingly fast. Unfortunately, as it soon turned out the enormous growth was not much more than a speculative bubble. The internet business collapsed dramatically in the year 2001. It was at that point when key players of the internet business like Tim O'Reilly and the company MediaLive International began to wonder whether the "dot-com collapse marked some kind of turning point for the web, such that a call to action like "Web 2.0" might make sense." [3] Since this turning point all online tools, which are used in an interactive, user-driven way, were labeled as "Web 2.0" applications. A large amount of consulting and internet companies worked hard to advertise the term "Web 2.0", yet failed most likely because the term "Web 2.0" was too artificial. Today, the term "Social Media Tools" is of increasingly accepted as it simply describes the tool's purpose better than the theoretical "Web 2.0" term.

2.3   The Term Social Web

Social webs are composed by individuals who are connected to each other. The connection can be used for different purposes such as personal and professional networking, information exchange, and updates. A social web should provide the following information about people:

- **Identity**: who are you? Depending on the purpose of the social web, different personal or professional aspects are of informative need.

- **Reputation**: what do people think you stand for? Within a social web, a user needs to create a personal or professional profile. Users try to create a preferred image of them that may differ from reality. The proper term for this phenomenon is "reputation management".

- **Presence**: where are you? Technologies geared toward the increase of a user's presence are currently growing on the internet market. A popular tool is called "Twitter" and is used for small status messages.

- **Relationships**: who are you connected with? Who do you trust? Connections between users describe personal or professional relationships. Most tools have the disadvantage in that they do not show the quality of the relationship.

- **Conversations**: what do you discuss with others? Conversations in social webs are performed in the same way as in direct inter-personal exchange. Forums and emails are the most important, and well-known media.

2.4   The Term Wiki

A wiki (the Hawaiian word for 'quick'), is a collaborative web site that allows virtually everybody to edit its pages. Usually, a website is created by a single person, team or company. Subsequently, the website's content is accessible to internet users around the globe. A wiki website is not created by a single person, team or company. Its base construct is created and published to the internet. As a consequence, every user has the possibility and the right to create, change or delete articles, pictures, and movies within a wiki page. Bo Leuf and Ward Cunningham have published a book called "The Wiki Way - Quick Collaboration on the Web." This title describes the phenomenon in a nutshell: Wikis are about collaboration. Users are working together on a central knowledge base, a base constituted by the user's collective knowledge, ergo the steep increase of contemporary discussion concerning the term "collective intelligence". [4]

2.5   Collective Intelligence

In James Surowiecki's seminal book *Swarm Intelligence – Why the Many are Smarter than the Few*, he explores a deceptively simple idea with profound implications: large groups of people are smarter than an elite few, no matter how brilliant this smaller group is, that is in their heightened ability to solving problems, fostering innovation, and making correct decisions.[5] In the context of wiki and the usage of social web tools, the increasing collaborative behavior of individuals is leading to a construct comparable to Surowiecki's notion of a collective intelligence.

3   Employee Development

Underlying my belief in the productivity of social web tools for companies is the conviction that it influences fundamentally and constructively the way a company's employees work within their professional circle. Or, as Malik has described, the advancement of employees should have the highest priority in people management tasks.[6]

3.1   Training

Employee training consists of various different disciplines. To ensure a qualitative and progressive working environment, employees need to be trained throughout their careers. John V.L. Morris highlights in his book *Employee Training* six different types of training in corporate training departments. Apprenticeship training is used during employee acquisition. Special training is used to learn for a specific operation or a special task. Intensive and part-time trainings are differentiated by the amount of time spent on the training. "Upgrade" and "promotion" trainings should render an employee capable of performing a more difficult task. So-called floor training is not a traditional training method. It is known as "learning on the job." [7] On-demand training is training "provided anytime, anywhere in the world when it is needed". [8]

3.2   Education

Employee education focuses upon the job that an individual may potentially hold in the future. One part of this process is to identify the potential of an individual, as well as this individual's possible future jobs. The other part is to set up a development plan for the individual. The reason why companies invest (or should invest) on employee education is well described by T. Davenport: "If we improve individual abilities to create, acquire, process, and use knowledge, we are likely to improve the performance of the processes individuals work on and the organizations they work for." [9]

3.3   Development

Employee development in particular is a process that is geared toward the preparation of employees for future job responsibilities. It also "prepares employees to keep pace with the organization as it changes and grows." [10]

A development plan has no specific and defined timeline. Although most companies set up annual development plans, Richard C. Grote proposes a much more aggressive plan. In his book *The Performance Appraisal* he states, that a week-by-week plan could help the development plan because it forces the individual to cut the development plan into manageable chunks.[11] Mondy states that in general "Training and Development (T&D) is the heart of a continuous effort designed to improve employee competency and organizational performance".[12]

3.4   Ramp-up

When a new employee joins the company, he/she has to accomplish a ramp-up phase in order to reach the standard and requirements of his/her colleagues within this company. During the ramp-up phase, every topic beneath the task employee development is facilitated. The individual has to process and acquaint him- or herself as quickly as possible with colleagues, his/her own work tasks, and the company's internal knowledge.

4   Employee Development using Social Media Tools

4.1   Training using Wiki based Knowledge Management

4.1.1   Why Knowledge Management

Dell, Grayson, and Essaides released a book in 1998 with the title *If We only Knew What we Know!* stating that "Knowledge Management (KM) is a conscious strategy of getting the right information to the right people at the right time so they can take action and create value."[12] Here, they indicate the importance of that on-demand availability of information and training material.

4.1.2   Knowledge Management using Wikis

As described in chapter 2.4, wikis are excellent tools for knowledge management. Since any article within a wiki is written by a company's employee, every article reflects the style, wording, and culture of the company. Furthermore, they allow employees to find specific information quickly and at any point in time. As Mondy puts it: "The ability to deliver knowledge to employees on an as-needed basis, anywhere on the globe, and at a pace consistent with their learning styles, greatly enhances the value of T&D." [10]

4.1.3   Reasoning

According to Mondy, Dell, Grayson, and Essaides any web-based knowledge management will enable a company to deliver knowledge and training on demand, and thus will leverage employees' readiness overall. Here, it is important to keep in mind that the Knowledge Management tool does not necessarily have to function as a social media tool. Quite the contrary, the most important function of the tool is the quality of the content so as to provide knowledge information.

4.2   Development using Social Webs

4.2.1   Networking as a Key Attribute

"Networking is an attribute of high performers" [9] – a clear statement provided by Davenport in his book *Thinking for a Living*. Here, he highlights the necessity of networking for employees leading them to be high performers and high potentials (known as HiPers and

HiPos) who are arguably the most valuable employees because they are very productive (HiPers) and have large potential for future productivity (HiPos).[13] Davenport's quote furthermore points to the fact that networking eventually helps to improve the productivity of all employees. If any of the employees would have the change to better manage their relations and connections to their colleagues (via networking tools), they increase their potential of being a HiPo or HiPer.

4.2.2   Networking for Career Boosts

Besides the performance and potential attributes for employees, there are also opportunities for employee development in terms of career development and planning. According to popular opinion, it is more important to know the right people, than to have extraordinary knowledge. Important career decisions often happen within a restaurant or a company party and neither in special assessment centers nor in a sophisticated selection processes. The fact that underlies this curious phenomenon is that it is in these instances (i.e. the restaurant) that social and professional exchange – and thus networking – takes place; Diane Darling released a book entitled *Networking for Career Success – 24 lessons for Getting to Know the Right People*.[14] This book, like many others on the market, emphasizes once more that the establishment of a solid network is the key for career success, and thus for the success of the company.

4.2.3   Networking using a Social Web

It is in the establishment of a solid network that social web tools play a significantly productive role. Chapter 2.3 highlighted the tasks of a social web tool which is to provide important information about and for its users. With this tool, employees should be able to create and manage a social network with other employees easier and more efficiently, thereby exchanging information, and thus increasing their performance, potential and career success. The German newspaper *Frankfurter Allgemeine Zeitung (FAZ)* conducted an experiment with a social web tool well-known within Germany. The tested social web tool is called "Xing" (http://www.xing.com) and accessible for everybody across the globe. This test points to issues a social media tool can entail. Although it is not a social web tool that was or is used internally within a company, it can be used as an example for the problems and limitations of a social web tool that is used internally within a company. The *FAZ* found in their test, that the tool is not used for career or employee development, but simply for advertisement and as a "singles club". Furthermore, the tool was found to give individuals the illusory impression of being close to the business, while in reality the contrary was the case. The harsh summary of the *FAZ* was that "XING" was a "big time wasting machine". [15]

4.2.4   Reasoning

This conclusion, while stressing an important point, is misleading when it comes to using social web tools in the context of a company where the proper advertisement and professional behavior would encourage employees to refrain from an all-too personal usage. Furthermore, a social media tool is first and foremost only a tool that can be used in a productive or destructive way. It's up to the employee, to use the tool given in the most effective and worthwhile way.

5   Issues and Limitations

5.1   Social Web Tools

The efficiency and productivity of social web tools are highly dependent of the way they are used by a company, and in extension by their employees. Advertised, framed, and applied in a productive and focused way, social web tools will leverage the employee's ability to connect and interact with other employees. The social web tools will help them to interact with their colleagues so as to improve their professional connections that will help improve not only their own, but also the company's efficient running.

The argument that these tools are used solely as a "single club" or "gossip exchange" distracts from the distinction that has to be made by personal and professional social web tools. To increase the professional usage of these tools, it is undoubtedly of high importance that the company will ensure this very usage. Company-intern social web tools, when designed and advertised as such, will have as clear and unmistaken guidelines to refrain from personal information, and instead use the tool for professional knowledge and information exchange.

5.2   Knowledge Management Tools

John Brown points in his book *The Social Life of Information* to the issue that IT (Information Technology) and the HR (Human Resources) factions tend to argue over the ownership of the knowledge management topic.[16] This issue, while presenting a valid concern, could be solved efficiently through a wiki where everyone would "own" the knowledge management system. The actual challenge is the content's quality of the knowledge management system, as any KM or wiki is only as good as its content.

5.3   Summary

As this paper has shown, social media tools can solve an immense amount of challenges within the employee development area. Used in a company-specific context and framework, these tools increase the knowledge exchange, promote the working culture within a company, and improve networking options. In this way they productively enhance the quality and quantity among employees contributing to the success of themselves and the company. However, one has to be aware of the disadvantages within the many advantages to avoid mistakes and an unproductive usage of these tools. For example a wiki based knowledge management system will stand and fall with the content's quality. Also, a social web tool will only provide support within a company if employees use the tool in a professional and serious manner. If social media tools for networking or knowledge management are not used as central communication and exchange platforms, they will decay to just some other time wasting intranet sites. Used properly and professionally for networking and knowledge management, social web tools entail yet another key to the success of a company and each of its individual employees.

6   Appendix - Sources:

1   Rusak, Sergey.
    http://www.progressiveadvertiser.com/web-2-0-becoming-an-outdated-term/
    Accessed: 11\19\2009
2   L. Lafko / D. Brake (2009)
    The Social Media Bible, Tactics, Tools, and Strategies for Business (p.52)
3   Tim O'Reilly (2005)
    http://oreilly.com/web2/archive/what-is-web-20.html
    Accessed: 11\19\2009
4   A. Ebersbach / M. Glaser / R. Heigl / A Warta (2008)
    Wiki, Kooperation im Web (p.448)
5   J. Surowiecki (2004)
    The Wisdom of Crowds: Why the Many are Smarter than the Few. (n/a)
6   F. Malik (2007)
    Management. (p.72)
7   J.V.L. Morris (2008)
    Employee Training: A Study Of Education And Training Departments In Various Corporations. (p.XVII et seq)
8   D. Ellis (2008)
    The New School. (p.41-42)
9   Thomas H. Davenport (2005)
    Thinking for a Living. (p.111)
10 R.W. Mondy (2008)
    Human Resource Management (11th Edition) (p.198)
11 R.C. Grote (2002)
    The Performance Appraisal. (p.200)
12 Mondy, (p.203)
13 C.S. Dell / C.J. Grayson / N. Essaides (1998)
    If only We Knew what We Know. (p. n/a)
14 W.J. Rothwell / R.D. Jackson (2005)
    Career Planning and Succession Management. (p.13)
15 D. Darling (2005)
    Networking for Career Success, 24 lessons for Getting to Know the Right People. (p.10)
16 F. Weidelich (2009),
    http://www.faz.net/s/RubE2C6E0BCC2F04DD787CDC274993E94C1/Doc~EA2A8D45C
    B0F84EC287541A49829576EF~ATpl~Ecommon~Scontent.html
    Accessed: 12/12/2009
17 J.S. Brown (2002)
    The Social Life of Information. (p.118)